FAKE•BOOK

HITS OF THE '90s

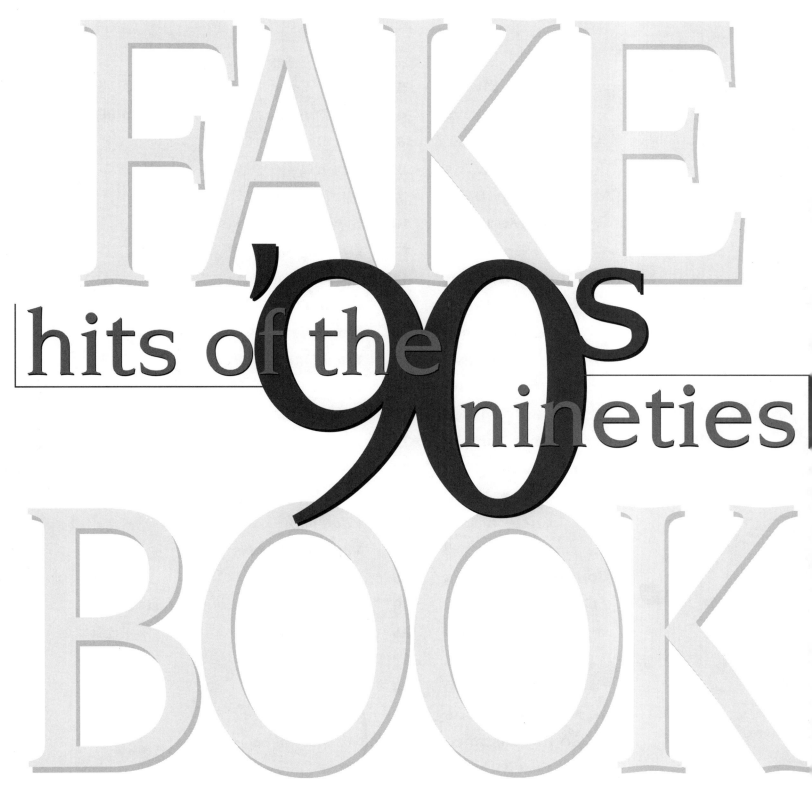

ISBN 0-7935-8886-3

HAL•LEONARD® CORPORATION

7777 W. BLUEMOUND RD. P.O. BOX 13819 MILWAUKEE, WI 53213

Visit Hal Leonard Online at
www.halleonard.com

ENTS

4

ALL FOR LOVE

from Walt Disney Pictures' THE THREE MUSKETEERS

Words and Music by BRYAN ADAMS,
ROBERT JOHN "MUTT" LANGE and MICHAEL KAMEN

ALL BY MYSELF

Music by SERGEI RACHMANINOFF
Words and Additional Music by ERIC CARMEN

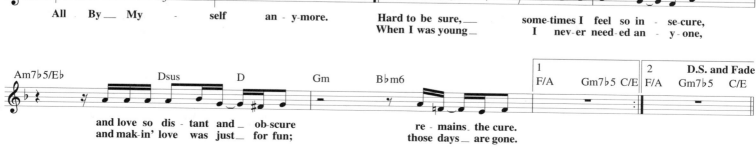

ALL THAT SHE WANTS

Words and Music by buddha,
joker, jenny and linn

ALWAYS BE MY BABY

Words and Music by MARIAH CAREY,
JERMAINE DUPRI and MANUEL SEAL

ALWAYS

Words and Music by
JON BON JOVI

As I Lay Me Down

Words and Music by
SOPHIE B. HAWKINS

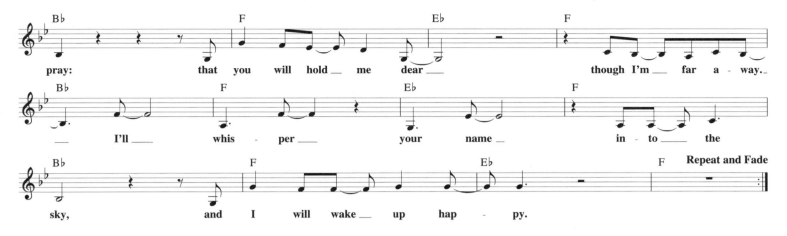

pray: that you will hold __ me dear __ though I'm __ far a - way. _

__ I'll __ whis - per __ your name __ in - to __ the

Repeat and Fade

sky, and I will wake __ up hap - py.

BEAUTIFUL IN MY EYES

Words and Music by
JOSHUA KADISON

Moderately (not too fast)

You're my peace _ of mind _ in this cra - zy world. _ You're ev - 'ry-thing I've
The world _ will turn _ and the sea - sons will change, and all the les - sons
lines up - on __ my face _ from a life-time of smiles, when the time comes

tried to _ find. _ Your love is a pearl. _ You're my
we will learn _ will be beau - ti - ful and strange. _ We'll have our
to em - brace _ for one long last while; _ we can

Mo - na Li - sa, you're my __ rain - bow skies, _ and my __ on - ly prayer _ is that you _
fill of tears, _ our _ share _ of sighs. My __ on - ly prayer _ is that you _
laugh a - bout _ how time _ real - ly flies. _ We won't _ say _ good - bye _ 'cause true love _

[1]
_ re - al - ize _ you'll al - ways be _ Beau-ti-ful In My Eyes.
_ re - al - ize _
_ nev - er dies; _

[2,3]
Eyes. You will al - ways

be Beau - ti - ful In My Eyes. _ And the pass-ing years will show _ that you will al - ways

To Coda
D.C. al Coda
(Take 2nd ending)
grow _ ev - er more Beau - ti - ful In My Eyes. When there are

CODA
Eyes. The pass - ing years will show _ that you will al - ways grow _ ev - er more Beau - ti - ful _

In My Eyes.

BARELY BREATHING

Words and Music by
DUNCAN SHEIK

BEAUTY AND THE BEAST
from Walt Disney's BEAUTY AND THE BEAST
(as performed by Celine Dion and Peabo Bryson)

Lyrics by HOWARD ASHMAN
Music by ALAN MENKEN

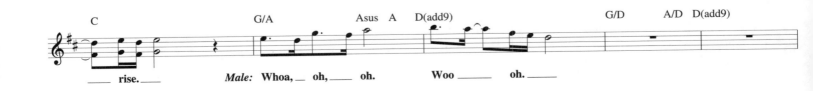

BED OF ROSES

Words and Music by
JON BON JOVI

Moderately slow

Sit - ting here   wast - ed and wound - ed   at this old   pi - an - o   try - ing
i - ron - clad   fist   I wake up   and French kiss   the morn - ing   while some
so far away   that each   step that   I take is on   my way home.   A king's

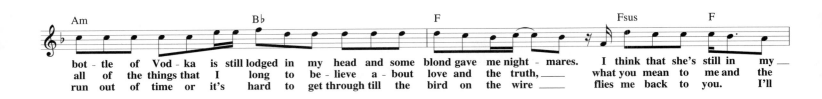

hard ___ to cap - ture the mo - ment   this morn - ing I   don't ___ know. ___   'Cause a
march - ing band keeps its own beat ___ in   my head while we're   talk - ing ___   a - bout
ran - som in dimes I'd give each night   to see through this   pay - phone. ___   Still I

bot - tle of Vod - ka is still lodged in   my head and some blond gave me night - mares.   I think that she's still in my ___
all of the things that I long to be - lieve a - bout love and the truth, ___   what you mean to me and the
run out of time or it's hard to get through till the bird on the wire ___   flies me back to you. I'll

1

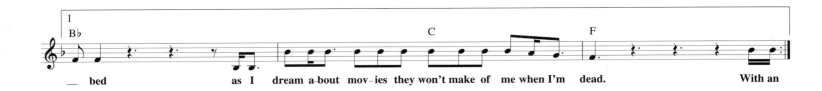

___ bed   as I dream a - bout mov - ies they won't make of me when I'm dead.   With an

2,3

truth is   ba - by, you're all that I ___ need. ___
just close my eyes   and whis - per,   "Ba - by,   blind love is ___   true."   I want to lay ___ you down on a Bed Of

Ros - es ___   for to - nite ___   I sleep on a bed of nails.   Oh, I want to be   just as close ___ as ___ the

To Coda ⊕   **D.C. al Coda**

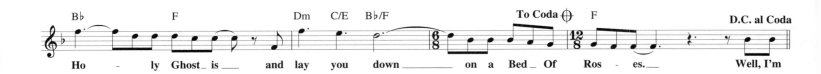

Ho - ly Ghost ___ is   and lay you down ___   on a Bed ___ Of Ros - es.   Well, I'm

BELIEVE

Words and Music by ELTON JOHN
and BERNIE TAUPIN

CANDLE IN THE WIND 1997

Music by ELTON JOHN
Words by BERNIE TAUPIN

BUTTERFLY KISSES

Words and Music by RANDY THOMAS
and BOB CARLISLE

CIRCLE OF LIFE
(as performed by ELTON JOHN)

Music by ELTON JOHN
Music by TIM RICE

COLORS OF THE WIND
from Walt Disney's POCAHONTAS
(as performed by VANESSA WILLIAMS)

Music by ALAN MENKEN
Lyrics by STEPHEN SCHWARTZ

CAN YOU FEEL THE LOVE TONIGHT
from Walt Disney Pictures' THE LION KING
(as performed by ELTON JOHN)

Music by ELTON JOHN
Lyrics by TIM RICE

END OF THE ROAD
from the Paramount Motion Picture BOOMERANG

Words and Music by BABYFACE,
L.A. REID and DARYL SIMMONS

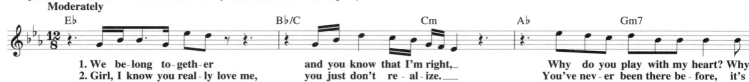

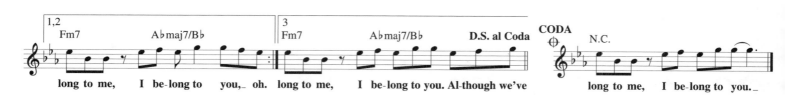

Additional Lyrics

(Spoken:) Girl, I'm here for you.
All those times at night when you just hurt me,
And just ran out with that other fellow,
Baby, I know about it.
I just didn't care.
You just don't understand how much I love you, do you?
I'm here for you.
I'm not out to go out there and cheat all night just like you did, baby.
But that's alright, huh, I love you anyway.
And I'm still gonna be here for you 'til my dyin' day, baby.
Right now, I'm just in so much pain, baby.
'Cause you just won't come back to me, will you?

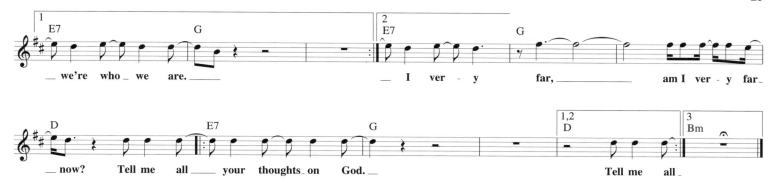

— we're who we are. ___ ___ I ver-y far, _____ am I ver-y far _
___ now? Tell me all ___ your thoughts on God. __ Tell me all _

FOREVER IN LOVE

By KENNY G

DON'T KNOW MUCH

Words and Music by BARRY MANN,
CYNTHIA WEIL and TOM SNOW

GROW OLD WITH ME

Words and Music by
JOHN LENNON

GIVE ME ONE REASON

Words and Music by
TRACY CHAPMAN

Medium Blues

G / C / D / G
Give Me One Rea-son to stay here and I'll turn right back a - round. _

C / D / G
Give Me One Rea-son to stay here _ and I'll turn right back a - round. _ Said I

D / C / G
don't want to leave you _ lone - ly; _ you _ got to make me change my _ mind. _

% / C / D / G
Ba-by, I got your num - ber. _ Oh, and I know that you got mine. _ But
want no one to squeeze me. They might take a - way my life. _ I don't
youth - ful heart can love you. Yes, and give you what you need. _ I said this
Ba-by, just Give Me One Rea - son. Oh, give me just one rea - son why.

C / D / G
you know that I called you. I called too man-y times. _ You can
want no one to squeeze me. They might take a - way my life. _ I just
youth - ful heart can love you, oh, and give you what you need. _ But I'm
Ba-by, just Give Me One Rea - son. _ Oh, give me just one rea-son why _ I _ should stay. Said I

D / To Coda ⊕ | 1-3 C / G
call me, ba - by. You can call me an - y - time. _ But you got to call _ me.
want some-one to hold me, oh, and rock me through the night. _
too old to go chas-ing you a - round, wast-ing my pre - cious en - er - gy. _
told you that I loved you, _

C / D / G
(1., 3.) Give Me One Rea-son to stay here _ and I'll turn right back a - round. _ (You could see me turn-ing.)
(2nd time - Instrumental solo)

C / D / G
Give Me One Rea-son to stay here _ and I'll turn back a - round. _ (You could see me turn-ing.) Said I

Repeat 2 times
then D.S. al Coda

D / C / G
don't want to leave you _ lone - ly; _ you _ got to make me change my _ mind. _ *(1st x only)* I don't
Solo ends This

CODA

⊕ C N.C. / G7
and there ain't no more to say. _

HAVE I TOLD YOU LATELY

Words and Music by
VAN MORRISON

Slowly, with expression

Have I Told You Late-ly that I love you? Have I told you there's no one else a-bove you?

Fill my heart with glad-ness, take a-way all my sad-ness,

ease my trou-bles that's what you do. For the morn-in' sun in all it's glo-
Instrumental

-ry greets the day with hope and com-fort, too. You fill my life with laugh-ter

and some-how you make it bet-ter, ease my trou-bles that's what you do.
Solo ends

There's a love that's di-vine and it's yours and it's mine like the sun.

And at the end of the day we should give thanks and pray to the one, to the one. Have I

to the one. And Have I Told You Late-ly that I love you? Have I

told you there's no one else a-bove you? You fill my heart with glad-ness,

take a-way my sad-ness, ease my trou-bles that's what you do.

Take a-way all my sad-ness, fill my life with glad-ness, ease my trou-bles that's what you

do. Take a-way all my sad-ness, fill my heart with glad-ness,

ease my trou-bles that's what you do.

HERE AND NOW

Words and Music by TERRY STEELE
and DAVID ELLIOT

Slowly

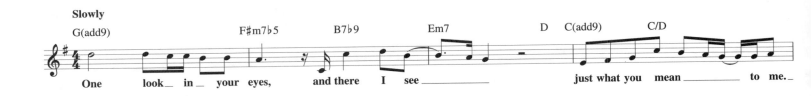

One look_ in _ your eyes, and there I see _____ just what you mean _____ to me._

_ Here_ in _ my heart I be-lieve _____ your love is all _____ I ev-er need._

Hold-ing you close_ through the night, _____ I need _ you. _____ Yeah. _____

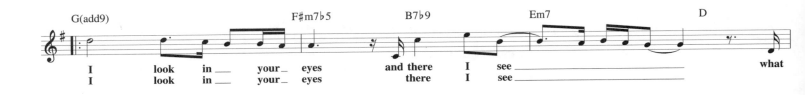

I look in __ your_ eyes and there I see _____ what
I look in __ your_ eyes there I see _____

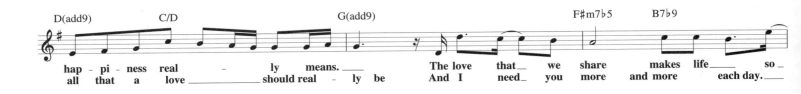

hap-pi-ness real ___ ly means. ____ The love that_ we share makes life _____ so_
all that a love _____ should real - ly be And I need_ you more and more each day. ___

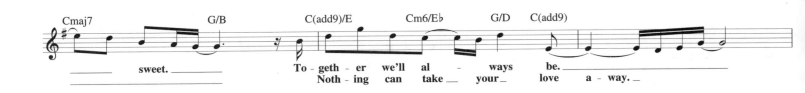

_____ sweet. _____ To-geth-er we'll al - ways be. _____
_____ Noth-ing can take __ your_ love a-way. __

This pledge of love ___ feels so right,_ and _ ooh, _____ I need _____ you. _____
More than ah - just ___ a dream. _____ I need _____ you. _____

GO THE DISTANCE

from Walt Disney Pictures' HERCULES
(as performed by MICHAEL BOLTON)

Music by ALAN MENKEN
Lyrics by DAVID ZIPPEL

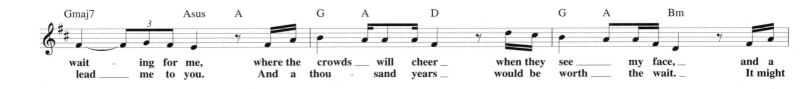

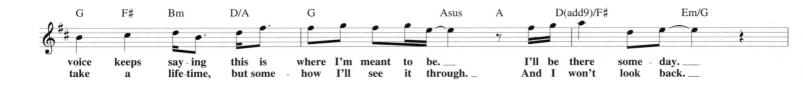

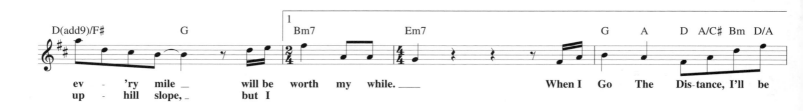

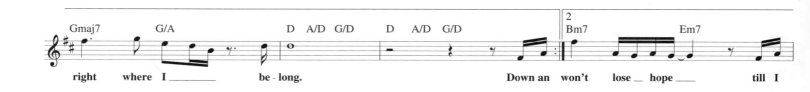

HONEY

Words by MARIAH CAREY
Music by MARIAH CAREY, SEAN "PUFFY" COMBS, KAMAAL FAREED,
STEVEN A. JORDAN, STEPHEN HAGUE, BOBBY ROBINSON,
RONALD LARKINS, LARRY PRICE and MALCOLM McLAREN

HOW AM I SUPPOSED TO LIVE WITHOUT YOU

Words and Music by MICHAEL BOLTON
and DOUG JAMES

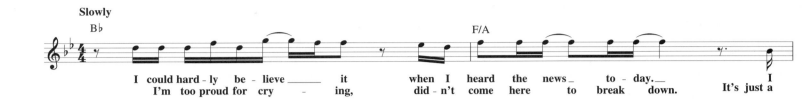

I could hard - ly be - lieve ___ it when I heard the news ___ to - day.
I'm too proud for cry - ing, did - n't come here to break down. It's just a I

had to come ___ and get it straight from you. ___ They said you are leav - in', some - one's
dream of mine ___ is com - in' to ___ an end. ___ And how can I blame ___ you when I

swept your heart ___ a - way. ___ From the look up - on ___ your face I see it's true. ___ So
built my world ___ a - round ___ the hope that one ___ day we'd be so much more than friends? ___

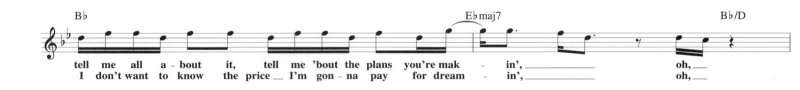

tell me all a - bout it, tell me 'bout the plans you're mak - in', ___ oh, ___
I don't want to know the price ___ I'm gon - na pay for dream - in', ___ oh, ___

tell me one thing more ___ be - fore ___ I go. ___ Tell me How Am I ___ Sup - posed ___ To Live ___ With - out ___
e - ven now it's more ___ than I can take. ___

___ You, ___ now that I've been ___ lov - in' you ___ so long? ___

How Am I ___ Sup - posed ___ To Live ___ With - out ___ You? And how am I ___ sup - posed ___ to car - ry on

I BELIEVE

Words and Music by JEFFREY PENCE,
ELIOT SLOAN and MATT SENATORE

Moderately, not too fast

Walk blind - ly to ____ the light ___ and reach out for ____ his hand.
Vi - o - lence has spread ___ world wide and there's fam - 'lies on ____ the street.
I've been see - ing Lis - a now for a lit - tle o - ver a year.

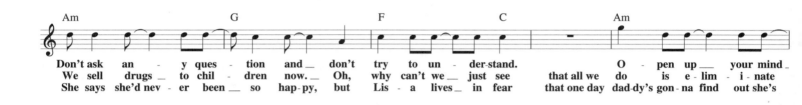

Don't ask an - y ques - tion and ___ don't try to un - der-stand. O - pen up ___ your mind ___
We sell drugs ___ to chil - dren now. ___ Oh, why can't we ___ just see that all we do is e - lim - i - nate
She says she'd nev - er been ___ so hap - py, but Lis - a lives ___ in fear that one day dad - dy's gon - na find out she's

___ and ___ then o - pen up ___ your heart, and you will see ___ that you ___ and me aren't
our fu - ture with things we do ___ to - day? Mon - ey is our in - cen - tive now, ___ so
in love with a nig - ger from ___ the streets. Oh, how he ___ would lose ___ it then, ___ but

To Coda ⊕

ver - y far a - part. ____ 'Cause But I Be - lieve _____ that love is ___ the an -
that makes it ___ o - kay. ____
she's still here ___ with me. ____

[1]
- swer. I Be - lieve _____ that love will find ___ a way. ___

[2]
___ I ___ Be - lieve _____ that love is ___ the an - swer. I Be - lieve ____

___ love will find ___ a way. ___

I BELIEVE IN YOU AND ME
from the Touchstone Motion Picture THE PREACHER'S WIFE

Words and Music by DAVID WOLFERT
and SANDY LINZER

Slow Ballad

I Be-lieve In You _ And Me. _____ I be-lieve that we will be _____ in love e-ter-nal-ly. _____ Well, as

far as I _ can see, you will al-ways be the one ____ for me, _____ oh, yes, you

will. And I be-lieve in dreams_ a-gain. _____ I be-lieve that love will nev-er end. _____ And

like the riv-er finds ____ the sea, I ____ was lost, _____ now I'm _

free _____ 'cause I Be-lieve_ In You_ And Me. I will nev-er leave_ your side. _ I will nev-er hurt

_ your _ pride. ____ When all the chips are down,_ babe, then I will al-ways be _ a-round.

Just to be right where you are, ___ my love. ____ You know I love _ you, boy. _ I'll nev-er

HERO

Words and Music by MARIAH CAREY
and WALTER AFANASIEFF

I CAN LOVE YOU LIKE THAT

Words and Music by STEVE DIAMOND,
MARIBETH DERRY and JENNIFER KIMBALL

Moderate Ballad

I DON'T HAVE THE HEART

Words and Music by ALLAN RICH
and JUD FRIEDMAN

I'LL MAKE LOVE TO YOU

Words and Music by
BABYFACE

Instrumental ad lib. and Fade

I DON'T WANT TO WAIT

Words and Music by
PAULA COLE

I FINALLY FOUND SOMEONE
from THE MIRROR HAS TWO FACES

Words and Music by BARBRA STREISAND, MARVIN HAMLISCH,
R.J. LANGE and BRYAN ADAMS

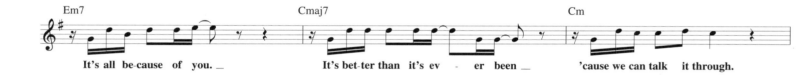

I KNOW

Lyric by MILTON DAVIS
Music by MILTON DAVIS and WILLIAM DUVALL

IF I EVER LOSE MY FAITH IN YOU

Written and Composed by
STING

IN THE HOUSE OF STONE AND LIGHT

Words and Music by
MARTIN PAGE

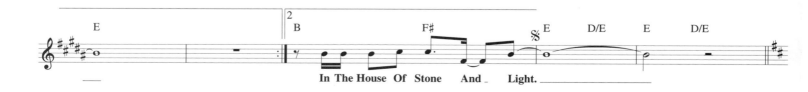

IT'S ALL COMING BACK TO ME NOW

Words and Music by
JIM STEINMAN

I'LL STAND BY YOU

Words and Music by CHRISSIE HYNDE,
TOM KELLY and BILLY STEINBERG

you, ___ I'll Stand By You. *(Instrumental)*

And when, when the night falls _

___ on you, ba - by, you're feel-ing all a - lone, you won't be on your own. I'll Stand By

You, I'll Stand By You, won't let no-bod-y hurt ___ you. ___ I'll Stand By

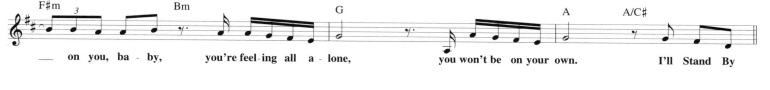

Repeat and Fade

You, take me in in-to your dark-est hour, ___ and I'll nev-er de-sert ___ you. ___ I'll Stand By

MISSION: IMPOSSIBLE THEME

By LALO SCHIFRIN

Moderately, with drive

LOVE OF A LIFETIME

Words and Music by BILL LEVERTY
and CARL SNARE

ONE SWEET DAY

Words and Music by MARIAH CAREY,
WALTER AFANASIEFF, SHAWN STOCKMAN,
MICHAEL McCARY, NATHAN MORRIS
and WANYA MORRIS

SOMEDAY

from Walt Disney's THE HUNCHBACK OF NOTRE DAME
(as performed by ALL-4-ONE)

Music by ALAN MENKEN
Lyrics by STEPHEN SCHWARTZ

SOMETHING ABOUT THE WAY YOU LOOK TONIGHT

Words and Music by ELTON JOHN
and BERNIE TAUPIN

TEARS IN HEAVEN

Words and Music by ERIC CLAPTON
and WILL JENNINGS

TO BE WITH YOU

Words and Music by ERIC MARTIN
and DAVID GRAHAME

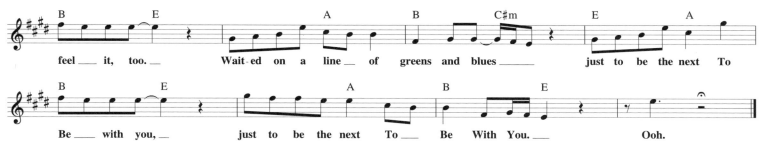

feel ___ it, too. ___ Wait-ed on a line ___ of greens and blues ___ just to be the next To

Be ___ with you, ___ just to be the next To ___ Be With You. ___ Ooh.

WATER RUNS DRY

Words and Music by
BABYFACE

Moderately

We don't e - ven talk an - y - more. ___ And we don't e - ven know what we ar -
Now they can see the tears in our eyes, ___ but we de - ny the pain that lies deep

gue a - bout. ___ Don't e - ven say, "I love you," no more, ___
in our hearts. ___ Well, may - be that's a pain we can't hide, ___

'cause say - in' how we feel is no long - er al - lowed. Some peo - ple will work
'cause ev - 'ry - bod - y knows that we're both torn a - part. ___ Why do ___ we hurt
Some peo - ple will work

___ things out ___ and some ___ just don't know ___ how to change. ___
___ each oth - er? Why do we push ___ love a - way? ___ Let's don't wait till the Wa - ter Runs Dry.
___ things out ___ and some ___ just don't know ___ how to change. ___

___ We might watch our whole lives ___ pass us by. ___ Let's don't wait till the Wa - ter Runs Dry. ___

___ We'll make the big - gest mis - take ___ of our lives. ___ Don't do it, ba - by. ___

To Coda ⊕

___ Ooh. ___ Na - ooh. ___

1.
2. **D.S. al Coda**

CODA

___ Don't do it, ba - by. ___ Ooh,

Na - ooh. ___ Don't do it, ba - by.

VISION OF LOVE

Words and Music by MARIAH CAREY
and BEN MARGULIES

WANNABE

Words and Music by MATT ROWE,
RICHARD STANNARD and SPICE GIRLS

WHERE DO YOU GO

Words and Music by G. MART,
PETER BISCHOF-FALLENSTEIN and JAMES WALLS

A WHOLE NEW WORLD

Aladdin's Theme
from Walt Disney's ALADDIN
(As performed by PEABO BRYSON and REGINA BELLE)

Music by ALAN MENKEN
Lyrics by TIM RICE

WHEN YOU SAY NOTHING AT ALL

Words and Music by DON SCHLITZ
and PAUL OVERSTREET

WHEN I FALL IN LOVE
featured in the TriStar Motion Picture SLEEPLESS IN SEATTLE

Words by EDWARD HEYMAN
Music by VICTOR YOUNG

When I Fall In Love it will be for-ev-er, ___ or I'll nev-er

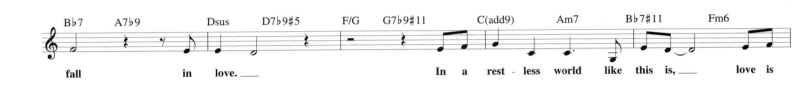

fall in love. ___ In a rest-less world like this is, ___ love is

end-ed be-fore it's be-gun, and too man-y moon-light kiss-es seem to cool in the warmth of ___ the

sun. When _ I give ___ my ___ heart ___ it will be ___ com -

- plete-ly, or ___ I'll nev - er give my heart. ___ Don't let me

give my heart. ___ And ___ the mo - ment I can feel ___ that _ you feel _ that ___ way

too, ___ I feel that _ way _ too, is When I Fall ___ In Love, I'll _ fall in love ___ with _ you. ___

WIND OF CHANGE

Words and Music by
KLAUS MEINE

Moderately slow

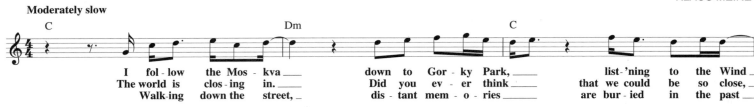

I fol - low the Mos - kva ___ down to Gor - ky Park, ___ list -'ning to the Wind
The world is clos - ing in. ___ Did you ev - er think ___ that we could be so close,
Walk - ing down the street, ___ dis - tant mem - o - ries ___ are bur - ied in the past ___

___ Of Change. ___ An Au - gust sum - mer night, ___ sol - diers pass - ing by, ___
___ like broth - ers? The fu - ture's in the air, ___ can feel it ev -'ry - where. ___
___ for - ev - er. I fol - low the Mos - kva ___ down to Gor - ky Park, ___

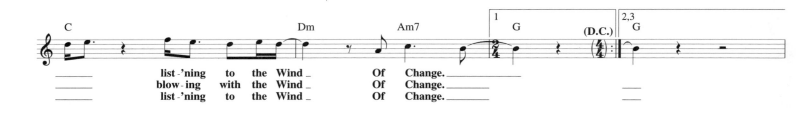

___ list -'ning to the Wind ___ Of Change. ___
___ blow - ing with the Wind ___ Of Change. ___
___ list -'ning to the Wind ___ Of Change. ___

(D.C.)

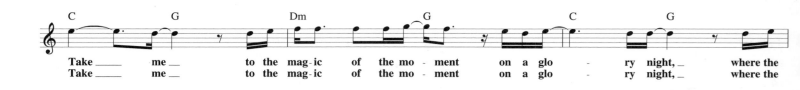

Take ___ me ___ to the mag - ic of the mo - ment on a glo - ry night, ___ where the
Take ___ me ___ to the mag - ic of the mo - ment on a glo - ry night, ___ where the

chil - dren of to - mor - row dream a - way ___ in the Wind Of Change. ___
chil - dren of to - mor - row share their dreams ___ for you and me. ___

To Coda

Mm. ___

D.C. al Coda

CODA

Take ___ me ___ to the

YOU MUST LOVE ME
from the Cinergi Motion Picture EVITA

Words by TIM RICE
Music by ANDREW LLOYD WEBBER

Additional Lyrics

Verse 2: *(Instrumental 8 bars)*
Why are you at my side?
How can I be any use to you now?
Give me a chance and I'll let you see how
Nothing has changed.
Deep in my heart I'm concealing
Things that I'm longing to say,
Scared to confess what I'm feeling
Frightened you'll slip away,
You must love me.